Think about it tomorrow, SNOOPY

Selected Cartoons from
Summers Fly, Winters Walk, Vol. 1

by CHARLES M. SCHULZ

D1211367

FAWCETT CREST • NEW YORK

A Fawcett Crest Book

Published by Ballantine Book

Contents of Book: PEANUTS ® Comic Strips by
Charles M. Schulz
Copyright © by United Feature
Syndicate Inc.

ISBN 0-449-20454-5

This book comprises a portion of SUMMERS FLY, WINTERS
WALK and is reprinted by arrangement with Holt, Rinehart
and Winston, Inc.

Manufactured in the United States of America

First Fawcett Crest Edition: February 1980
First Ballantine Books Edition: September 1983

Think about it tomorrow, SNOOPY

MARCIE, YOU'RE REALLY NOT INTERESTED IN BASEBALL, ARE YOU?

I HATE BASEBALL, SIR.. I ONLY PLAY ON YOUR TEAM TO AVOID OFFENDING YOU

WELL, WHY DON'T YOU GET BACK OUT THERE AT SHORTSTOP, AND OFFEND A FEW OF THOSE GROUND BALLS?

YOU MANAGERS HAVE A COLORFUL WAY OF TALKING, SIR!

SIR, HOW COME EVERYONE ON CHUCK'S TEAM HAS A CAP, BUT WE DON'T?

THEY'RE A BUNCH OF LOSERS, MARCIE! WHICH WOULD YOU RATHER HAVE, A WINNING TEAM OR A CAP?!

WINNING DOESN'T MEAN THAT MUCH TO ME, SIR... I'D RATHER HAVE A CAP

YOU'RE WEIRD, MARCIE!!

SCHULZ

HEY, CHUCK, I HAVE TO ASK YOU SOMETHING..

EVERYONE ON MY TEAM SUDDENLY THINKS WE NEED BASEBALL CAPS...WHERE DID YOU GUYS GET YOURS?

WE JUST WENT OUT AND BOUGHT THEM OURSELVES...

ALL EXCEPT OUR SHORTSTOP... HE GOT HIMSELF A SPONSOR!

JOE'S PET SHOP

SCHULZ

MARCIE! LISTEN TO THIS...

"KIDS' DAY AT BALL PARK...CHILDREN ADMITTED FREE, AND EACH CHILD TO RECEIVE SOUVENIR BASEBALL CAP."......THAT'S IT, MARCIE!

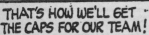

THAT'S HOW WE'LL GET THE CAPS FOR OUR TEAM!

YOU DON'T CARE FOR MY LATEST DESIGN, HUH, SIR?

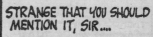

HEY, CAT! I DON'T REALLY APPRECIATE THIS NICK YOU PUT IN MY DOGHOUSE!

BUT I'M GONNA FORGIVE YOU! YOU WANNA KNOW WHY I FORGIVE YOU?

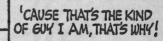

'CAUSE THAT'S THE KIND OF GUY I AM, THAT'S WHY!

JUST DON'T ASK TO BORROW ANY OF MY JONI JAMES RECORDS AGAIN!

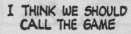

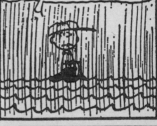

HEY, LOOK! YOUR BROTHER IS FLOATING OUT TO SEA ON THE PITCHER'S MOUND!

YOU SHOULD WAVE TO HIM...YOU'LL PROBABLY NEVER SEE HIM AGAIN...

SO LONG, BROTHER!

WHO'S GOING TO FEED THE DOG?

YES, MA'AM... SOMEBODY STOLE MY LUNCH BOX!

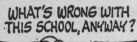

WHAT'S WRONG WITH THIS SCHOOL, ANYWAY?

I FEEL LIKE I'M SURROUNDED BY PIRATES

THIS PLACE IS GETTING TO BE A REGULAR BLACKBEARD JUNGLE!

I SHOULD THINK YOU'D DO BETTER IF YOU JOGGED ALONG THE SIDE OF THE ROAD SOMEWHERE

THAT'S TOO DANGEROUS...

PEOPLE RUN OUT AND BITE ME!

THESE ARE DITTOS!

THESE ARE DITTOS CHASING DOTTOS INTO GROTTOES! AND THESE ARE LOTTOS QUOTING MOTTOES TO BLOTTOS!

YOU'RE JUST JEALOUS BECAUSE I ENJOY MY HOMEWORK!

ALL RIGHT, EVERYBODY PAY ATTENTION!

WE'RE ALL GOING TO SLEEP... HEAD, FEET, STOMACH, ARMS, LEGS AND EARS... THAT MEANS NO MIDNIGHT SNACKS AND NO RUNNING AROUND!

HEE HEE HEE

AND NO GIGGLING!

SCHULZ

TELL YOUR CATCHER THAT THE GIRLS IN THE OUTFIELD HAVE JUST VOTED HIM AS THE CUTEST THING THIS SIDE OF HEAVEN!

HEY, CATCHER! THE GIRLS IN THE OUTFIELD HAVE JUST VOTED YOU AS THE CUTEST THING THIS SIDE OF HEAVEN!

HE SAID, "THANK YOU"

HE ALSO SAYS MAYBE YOU SHOULD PLAY A LITTLE DEEPER... MOVE BACK A LITTLE...

LIKE MAYBE FIFTY MILES!!

SCHULZ

I'VE BEEN THINKING ABOUT SOMETHING..

CHUCK, HAVE YOU EVER TOLD A GIRL THAT YOU LIKE HER?

AND HAVE HER LAUGH IN MY FACE? NOTHING DOING!!

IT HURTS TO HAVE YOUR FACE LAUGHED IN

I DON'T UNDERSTAND CHUCK..

WELL, SAY SOMETHING NICE TO ME, AND I'LL SHOW YOU...

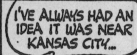

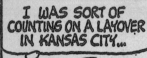

ARE YOU SURE YOU WANT TO PLAY AT WIMBLEDON?

YOU'D PROBABLY COME UP AGAINST PLAYERS LIKE ASHE, OR CONNORS, OR OKKER OR BORG...

THAT'S TRUE...I HATE PLAYING GUYS LIKE THAT

THEY KEEP HITTING THE BALL BACK!

WHERE WILL YOU STAY IF YOU GO TO ENGLAND?

YOU DON'T KNOW ANYONE THERE

WHY CAN'T I STAY DOWNSTAIRS WITH MR. HUDSON AND MRS. BRIDGES?

BETTER YET, I'LL STAY UPSTAIRS WITH MISS GEORGINA!

YOU'RE LEAVING FOR WIMBLEDON NOW?

BUT IT'S THE MIDDLE OF THE NIGHT!!

YOU ALWAYS LEAVE FOR WIMBLEDON AT NIGHT... IF YOU LOSE IN THE FIRST ROUND, NO ONE WILL EVER KNOW

THAT DOG OF MINE CAUSES ME MORE WORRY!

NOW, HE'S OFF TO WIMBLEDON...AT LEAST HE THINKS HE'S OFF TO WIMBLEDON...HE DOESN'T EVEN KNOW WHERE IT IS!

HOW IN THE WORLD DOES HE THINK HE'S GOING TO GET THERE?

♪ I BEEN WORKIN' ON THE RAILROAD... ♪

SCHULZ

HERE'S SOMETHING INTERESTING..

"AUTHORITIES REPORTED TODAY THE FINDING OF A TENNIS RACKET FIVE MILES EAST OF TOWN NEAR THE RAILROAD TRACKS...FOUL PLAY IS SUSPECTED"

"NO FINGERPRINTS WERE PRESENT, BUT SMUDGES SIMILAR TO PAW PRINTS WERE ON THE RACKET"

"AUTHORITIES ADMITTED TO BEING PUZZLED"

I CAN'T STAND IT...

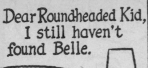
Dear Roundheaded Kid, I still haven't found Belle.

I am writing this letter in a store that sells typewriters.

Right now, a clerk is eyeing me rather suspiciously.

WHAT'S THE MATTER? DON'T I LOOK LIKE A CUSTOMER?

BELLE? BELLE?

HOW AM I EVER GOING TO FIND BELLE?

THE LAST I HEARD SHE HAS A TEEN-AGE SON, AND THAT WORTHLESS HOUND SHE MARRIED RAN OFF!

"I GUESS I FORGOT TO TELL YOU THAT BELLE IS MY SISTER...IF IT TURNS OUT THAT SHE NEEDS HELP, WILL YOU SEND SOME MONEY?"

MONEY? I DON'T HAVE ANY MONEY!

HE'S YOUR DOG, CHARLIE BROWN!

BELLE ALWAYS LIKED THE WATER...

I'LL BET IF I GO DOWN TO THE OCEAN AND JUST HANG AROUND, I'LL RUN INTO HER...

"AND SO I WALKED CLEAR AROUND KANSAS CITY, BUT I NEVER FOUND THE OCEAN...THIS HAS BEEN A VERY DISCOURAGING DAY"

AND NOW, I CAN'T EVEN REMEMBER WHY I'M WEARING THIS TENNIS VISOR!

ANOTHER LETTER FROM SNOOPY?

"DEAR ROUND-HEADED KID... GUESS WHAT HAPPENED!"

"I FOUND MY SISTER BELLE... AND WHAT A REUNION WE'RE HAVING! BELLE IS JUST AS BEAUTIFUL AS EVER"

"UNFORTUNATELY, I CAN'T SAY MUCH FOR HER TEEN-AGE SON"

"BY THE TIME YOU RECEIVE THIS LETTER, I WILL BE ON A TRAIN HEADING FOR HOME"

"I GUESS I WON'T BE PLAYING AT WIMBLEDON AFTER ALL...I JUST HEARD THAT THEY STARTED WITHOUT ME"

ALL RIGHT FOR YOU GUYS!!

ARE YOU HAVING A GOOD TIME? ARE YOU SWINGING ANY BIG DEALS?

WHO ARE YOU CALLING?

WHAT?

I SAID, WHO ARE YOU CALLING? WHO IS THIS?

CHUCK! WHAT ARE YOU DOING THERE?

I'M NOT THERE... I'M HERE! I THINK YOU DIALED THE WRONG NUMBER...

CHUCK, YOU ALWAYS SPOIL EVERYTHING!!

I SUPPOSE SOMEDAY WHEN I GET TO BE A FATHER, IT'LL BE EVEN WORSE...

"WHO SHUT IN THE SEA WITH DOORS WHEN IT BURST FORTH FROM THE WOMB? HAVE YOU ENTERED THE STOREHOUSE OF THE SNOW?"

"WHO CAN NUMBER THE CLOUDS BY WISDOM? OR WHO CAN TILT THE WATERSKINS OF THE HEAVENS?"

"IS THE WILD OX WILLING TO SERVE YOU? DO YOU GIVE THE HORSE HIS MIGHT? IS IT BY YOUR WISDOM THAT THE HAWK SOARS, AND SPREADS HIS WINGS TOWARD THE SOUTH?"

DON'T CRITICIZE THE WORLD, CHARLIE BROWN

HOW WOULD IT BE IF I JUST YELLED AT THE UMPIRE?

ARE YOU GOING TO SPEND YOUR WHOLE SUMMER WATCHING TV?

NO, I'VE DECIDED TO GO OVER TO OUR LOCAL LIBRARY, AND SIGN UP FOR A COURSE IN FRENCH LITERATURE!

HAHAHAHA!!

NOW, MY STOMACH IS GOING TO HURT FOR THE REST OF THE DAY...